OneNote

The Ultimate Guide to OneNote - Goals, Time Management & Productivity

By: Alex Downey

has been made to provide accurate, up to date and reliable complete information. No warranties of any kind are expressed or implied. Readers acknowledge that the author is not engaging in the rendering of legal, financial, medical or professional advice.

By reading this document, the reader agrees that under no circumstances are we responsible for any losses, direct or indirect, which are incurred as a result of the use of information contained within this document, including, but not limited to, — errors, omissions, or inaccuracies.

Table of Contents

Introduction

Welcome to the Ultimate Guide to OneNote (Goals, Time, Management & Productivity). This short book will tell you all you need to know about a Microsoft Office application that's been around for a while and yet, for some reason, not too many people know about it or use it.

The application I am talking about is OneNote, and by the time you are finished reading this book, you should become aware that you've been missing on a very neat little piece of software that is not only highly useful but is also completely free!

I've been around computers for years, so I am well aware of what most of you are thinking right now. Right, yet another application, just what I need. Not! And I understand the sentiment completely. With so many software "solutions" that we are being attacked with on a daily basis, it really seems that software developers these days don't actually care about the quality of the product. Their MO is more along the lines, let's put it out there and see if people budge. If they don't, we'll just put out a new one. Rinse and repeat. It can get quite frustrating over time.

However, OneNote is truly different. Although it looks much like a standard Microsoft Office application, its main goal is to become personal for every individual user. Unlike other apps that force you to learn how to handle them, OneNote gives you as much creative freedom as possible when it comes to application software.

Things in this world of ours are changing rapidly. The pace of everyday personal and, even more, professional life is easily ten times faster than it used to be twenty years ago. Keeping up with everything, staying in the loop, and not losing your mind is a real challenge. From friends and family to school and work, we need to get more and more things done on a daily basis. Since this push is largely thanks to the technology, why not use that same technology to help us cope?

And that's the core idea of OneNote. It was designed to be your personal electronic notebook, in which you enter all sorts of notes, from shopping lists to those relating to serious business projects. A regular, old-fashioned notebook simply doesn't cut it anymore. Most information we gather these days comes from electronic sources and primarily the world wide web.

We spend a bulk of our time in offices and at home in front of a computer. We read the news online, we do our research online, and more and more we read our books on electronic devices. In line with that, we need an electronic notebook to catch the notes as we go, without stopping what we are doing.

The creators of OneNote really did their best to make the software as similar as possible to an actual notebook. The restrictions are indeed minimal, you can put in all sorts of information, and it also supports handwriting and drawing. It is the amount of freedom unparalleled in the software world.

The pages that follow will tell you all you need to know about OneNote. I will explain what this program does in detail, describe its different functionalities, and explain some of its applications in the real world, using examples that every single one of us can relate to. It may sound a bit too much to expect from a simple application, but OneNote can truly improve your life quality on so many levels once you learn to use it properly.

We'll start out by diving into what OneNote is and take a look at what kind of variations are present in different versions that have come out over the years. Next, we'll take a look at how OneNote can be integrated into your life and how you can take advantage of it no matter which walk of life you belong to.

The final chapter will also offer some advice on what cheap devices you could get to run this software. There are some really inexpensive laptops and tablets out there that can handle all the tasks described in this book with ease. We'll end the entire book with a large glossary of shortcuts that you can use to streamline your daily life, without having to refer to a search engine or using the help feature in the program.

In all honesty, although I've been a (heavy) computer user for more than twenty years, I've only learned about OneNote a few years back. It is just one of those applications that people don't talk about much. However, since finding it, I've realized just how much it can help you deal with everyday tasks and significantly reduce frustration levels.

So, without further ado, I give you OneNote.

Chapter 1
What Is OneNote, Exactly?

With a number of different application software solutions published nearly every day, it is often hard to keep track. More is usually better, but in the computer world, it can cause you not to be able to see the forest for the trees. It is an unfortunate fact (but the fact, nonetheless) that a lot of applications range from marginally useful to straightforward useless. And thus, the good stuff gets lost somewhere in the pile, never finding its way to the end-users.

OneNote is one such application. It's been a part of Microsoft Office package since 2007, and in 2013 the company made a version of the application available to everyone free of charge. So it is not only a great app to have, but it will not cost you a penny either.

So, what is OneNote? In the simplest words, it is a good, old fashion paper notebook, brought to you in an electronic form. And when I say it's just like a notebook, I really mean it.

Other applications, like Notepad or MS Word, are quite restrictive in terms of what you can do with text and how you can arrange it. OneNote offers all the freedom you could ever need. With a free-form canvas at your disposal, you can write, draw, add images and more. Whatever makes your life easier.

Some of us still remember what it was like to write down your notes on paper. From the basic information to complex (sometimes confusing, in all fairness) charts to make sure we have all the relevant info organized just as we like it. What works for someone can seem like a complete mess for someone else, but that is the whole point. You take notes for yourself, to make your life easier, and it needs to make sense to you.

Microsoft OneNote is a rather successful attempt to imitate all this in an electronic form. There is no right way or wrong way to take notes. You are free to experiment and see what works best for you personally. Develop your style as you go and change things in any manner you see fit. Unlike the majority of other applicative software, OneNote is for you and you alone. Nobody will ask to see your work, and you will not be sending the documents to your demanding clients. It is as personal as you want it to be and the only time anyone else will see it is when you are bragging to your friends about how well organized your life is thanks to OneNote.

The advantages of OneNote over a traditional notebook are quite a few. First of all, with how far the technology has advanced, you will never run out of space. Those notes can add pretty fast, and instead of having a bunch of different notebooks in your drawer, you will have it all in one place.

Secondly, the application makes all sorts of formatting very easy. You can make lists, tables, diagrams, and anything else that will potentially make your life easier. Sometimes it is all too easy to go crazy with it at the start, but you will find your groove after spending some time with the program.

Finally, OneNote works with all sorts of multimedia. By using containers to store the information, the application ensures that you can insert pretty much anything you like. Pictures, screenshots, information from the Internet or other programs, and even external files - OneNote can handle it all.

We will cover this in more detail in the next chapter, but navigating and handling the information inside the application is very simple. Everything can be edited, moved around, and merged. Notes can be tagged and searched, so if you ever have a hard time finding something you know is in there, a few simple words should help you get there. There is no need anymore to frantically go back and forth through all the pages, hoping you will spot what you are looking for.

Finally, it is very simple for more users to share the same Notebook (or a few of them). As long as you store the files in a shared location, anyone with access will be able to edit, add new notes, and make any necessary changes. In addition to storing the files in a shared location, you can also start a Live Sharing Session and send out invitations to your friends or coworkers straight to their email inboxes.

Once you get used to OneNote, you will have a hard time imagining your life without it. What's even better about it is that smart people from Microsoft realized that having an application for PCs and laptops is no longer enough, so they came up with apps for all major smartphone and tablet platforms, including Windows phones, iPhones and iPads and Androids.

Right about now, you are probably asking the same question I did when doing some research for this book, as it is a natural question to ask: do they sync? The answer, to our satisfaction, is yes, they do. Your notes will sync across the various platforms and devices, so you will always have the latest updates right there in your bag or pocket. And you will quickly learn to appreciate it.

Chapter 2
What's New with OneNote 2016?

To keep up with our changing needs, Microsoft keeps adding new and better features to their digital notebook. While all software is based on older versions and may seem familiar, OneNote 2016 adds tons of new features for capturing, storing and sharing all kinds of information. That being said, remember One Note is available for most devices and in a lot of different versions. So if you don't have one particular device, fret not, there's probably a version out there for you.

First, we're going to go through some of the newer features in the latest 2016 version as compared to older versions. As most Windows 10 users might be aware, there are two versions of OneNote on their device: OneNote and OneNote 2016. We'll dive into those differences a little later in this chapter. Familiarizing yourself with the version you are using will make you more efficient and help you save time.

The most obvious feature of OneNote 2016 is it's bolder, more colorful look versus the layout of 2013's version—except it has more added features when you look closely. Let's take a look at some of these newer features.

Embed videos from the web

You no longer need to save videos to your hard disk and upload them OneNote. You can now embed videos directly from YouTube, Vimeo or Office Mix.

Integrate with Microsoft Edge

Microsoft's newest and lightest browser joins up with OneNote to provide you with the ability to take notes on any web page. You can even highlight text on a page or share your notes and comments to OneNote and your other connections that are present there.

Mail yourself notes from anywhere

Want to save contents of your inbox to OneNote? Doing so is easier than ever before. Simply mail your note to me@onenote.com and you're good to go. You can send yourself on-the-go ideas you have had, simple reminders, or simply write a quick email. Inside the application, you can use the Email button to share any note with yourself or others.

New Clipper to capture anything online

OneNote Clipper has been around for some time. OneNote 2016 makes it simpler and more attractive than before. You can clip an entire page or just a part. Microsoft has also added a bookmark plug-in, so your Clipper is easily accessible to you as you browse online.

Office Lens integration

Office Lens is a mobile-only app by Microsoft. It's a great way to capture notes and information from your regular life. With its sharp quality, you don't need to worry about blurry images. It provides you with all your notes in one location. You can even capture sketches, drawing and equations—depending on your need. And now, you can send your Office Lens notes to your OneNote right from your cell phone. There's no lengthy process involved in integration, and you can access your notes from any place you need to.

These new features separate the old and the new. If you're using an older version, you'll still find yourself with a ton of features to work with. We'll discuss those in the coming chapters. Now, as discussed, Windows 10 users might see two versions of OneNote on their device, OneNote and OneNote 2016. The two applications are very similar, but there are a few key differences. OneNote is built from the ground up for seamless integration between all devices, while OneNote 2016 is the standard for your PC device. OneNote, as with most applications, will be continually updated with new features, while OneNote 2016, will run as a more classic software application. You can use either or both, depending on what you like.

Let's take a look at exclusive features provided in each application which makes them unique to one another.

Available only in OneNote for Windows 10

- View all your notes sorted by when you last updated them

- Preview your notes without having to open the page

- Transform your drawings into shapes automatically

- See who's working with you in a shared notebook and jump straight to the page they're on

- Windows 10 integration, including:

- Click the button on the Surface Pen to open OneNote and take a note, even when your device is locked

- Tell Cortana to take a note for you with your voice

- Quickly jump to a new page by selecting the Note button in the Action Center

- Write on a web page in Microsoft Edge and save your annotations to OneNote

- Share notes with any app with the Share button

- Use your device's camera to capture documents, whiteboards, receipts, and more right into OneNote

- Maximize drawing space by hiding the page list and Ribbon

Available only in OneNote 2016

- Capture a screen clipping (Win+Shift+S) and add it to your notes or the clipboard

- Print anything on your computer directly to OneNote

- Office suite integration, including:

- Insert meeting details from Outlook into your notes

- Insert an embedded Excel spreadsheet into your notes

- Create tasks in OneNote and have them appear in Outlook

- Convert handwriting into text

- Take notes during a recording and have OneNote will highlight what you were writing when you play back the recording later

- Use the equation editor to add complex equations to your notes

- Insert basic shapes from the Draw menu

- Categorize notes with custom tags and quickly find them later

- Apply a template to pages to maintain a specific look or layout

- Store notebooks on your local hard drive instead of in the cloud

Mac users and mobile users will find new features are added nearly every month, but the above standard features are mostly included in them. You'll be able to integrate with devices and use features only previously available on a certain device.

This book is written with regards to being helpful for any OneNote user—whether you're using OneNote 2010 or 2016. By knowing which version you're using, you'll be able to know where things are and what features you have at your disposal.

Chapter 3
OneNote 101

If you've ever worked in one of Microsoft applications, like Word or Excel (and the odds are, you have), you won't have much trouble finding your way around OneNote. Regardless, in this chapter, I will break down some of the essential functionalities and offer some explanation about how the program essentially operates.

As already noted, OneNote application can best be compared to a real-life tabbed notebook. For example, you may have (or have thought about starting) a journal to keep track of your business information and another one for your personal stuff.

With the application, you can do this very thing, e.g. you can start as many notebooks as you like and name them appropriately for easier navigation. Every new notebook will be stored in the OneNote folder by default, but you can change their location and move them around just like any other files.

The application window contains four main areas. To the left, there is the Navigation Bar, listing all the notebooks stored in the default location. It makes it easy for you to access any of them with a simple click. When in full view, the Bar displays the structure of each notebook. You can collapse the Navigation Bar to make more room for the content area.

The content panel occupies the central area of the window. It represents blank pages you can fill with content and add to your existing notebooks. Every page keeps track of the date and time of the latest modifications, so you don't have to worry about those details and can instead focus on adding the relevant information.

The other two areas of the window are the notebook header, enabling you to move between different sections in the notebook, and the Page tabs, which make it easy to move between the pages.

There is a neat little trick if you ever need to have more notebooks open at the same time. If you press Ctrl+M (hold down Ctrl and press M while still holding Ctrl), another instance of the OneNote window will pop out, without closing the current one.

Editing Notes

The text editing ribbon is much similar to the one in MS Word applications, but in OneNote is collapsed by default to provide more space for writing. Once you make it display, you will find the usual suspects under the headings: File, Home, Insert, Share, Review, and View plus an additional tab called Draw.

File tab contains the usual options for handling the files, like the opening, closing, saving, etc.

Under the Insert heading, you will find options enabling you to add external files, like images, audio and video, special symbols, etc.

Share tab contains all those options we mentioned in Chapter 1. If you need to share the notebook with your friends, family, or coworkers, you will find all you need right here.

Review options help you with fine combing your text, making sure that spelling and grammar are good, and you can also find some translation options for the supported languages. Depending on whether you share your files or not, you may never really need this particular tab.

View tab helps you switch between different appearances of the window or managing multiple windows at the same time.

Finally, the Draw tab contains tools that you can use to produce simple drawings or handwritten content if you ever require this.

Creating And Configuring Notebooks

Now that you have a basic idea of how it all works and what it looks like, it is time to take a quick glance at how you can create new notebooks and configure them to meet your exact needs.

If you need just a personal notebook, you can either do it from a scratch or use one of the ready-made templates that come with the program. Depending on the version you are using, you may or may not have templates available to you.

Either way, the creation of your first notebook is a rather straightforward process. Select New from the program menu and your document will be ready for editing, available to you to add pages and sections as you see fit. The exact structure will depend on your particular needs, but we will address that topic as well in the next chapters.

In order to make your notebook available to you at more than one location, you can store it in a shared folder on your network, save it to a USB drive that you can carry around with you, or store it online. Storing your data online probably makes the most sense in this day and age, where you want the access to your information available at all times.

If you use Microsoft SharePoint or OneDrive for your online storage, this will make it extremely easy for synchronization of the information across all your devices, regardless of how many you have. Once you are logged in with your personal account, the information will be refreshed every time you start OneNote on any device. There is no particular need to explain how useful this can be to anyone, from a housewife going out to buy some groceries to a high-level businessman who put together an elaborate plan on his home PC, but suddenly needs to access it from work.

Thanks to a really wide range of available functionalities, OneNote can be so much more than just a note taking application. You can use it for the initial layouts of plans, business proposals, and similar. In those circumstances, cooperation with other people involved becomes critical.

The application creators clearly had this in mind when they were making the software, as there is a very clear accent on collaboration. Making shared notebooks in which multiple people ("authors") can add, remove, and edit content is as easy as A, B, C.

You can start the project as a shared notebook or share the existing document at some point down the line. Either way, once an "author" access the shared notebook, a local copy will be created for them, so they can work on it even when not connected to the Internet. Once they connect, everything will be updated, as their edits will be added and they will receive all the edits made by other contributors.

OneNote keeps track of all the changes, with dates and names of the author. It also saves the previous versions, so you can always roll back to an earlier point in time before certain changes were made. This can be a real lifesaver at such times when something important goes missing by accident.

To share an existing notebook, click the File menu and select Share tab. You will have two options: to share it on your local network or the web. Depending on your work model, you can select an appropriate one. If you are working with other people who are members of the same network, then you can share it that way. If you all work from home or different offices, not on the same network, share it on the web and make access simple for everyone.

You will also have a nice little option to email everyone involved and send them the link to your newly shared notebook, making sure everybody gets the message.

Organizing Your Notebook

Whether you prefer to first create the structure and then add the content or vice versa is entirely up to you. OneNote lets you do both, so whatever you feel more comfortable with doing is fine.

When you first open a new notebook, it contains only one section and a single page. Adding new sections, pages, and subpages is very simple, and you can add as many as you like.

In order to make your life easy, you should stick to some general guidelines when it comes to organization. First of all, consider the type of information your notebook will contain and use this as your starting point. If for example, it is some sort of a customer records database, it is probably a good idea to add a new section for every client and then further divide the sections into relevant pages and subpages. More on this later.

Another important aspect to consider is the volume of information. As stated earlier, it is easy to get carried away and add all sorts of stuff on a page, but, ideally, you want to be able to visually access and understand all info on the page with a single glance. Don't let your pages get huge and make you scroll too much. If this happens, consider dividing them into subpages for easier and quicker access.

You can define the page size (A3 - A6, Letter, Legal, etc.) and background. There are some ready-made page templates for some typical applications, like academic templates (Lecture Notes of different varieties), business templates (for projects, meeting notes, etc.), and planner templates (several types of To Do lists).

When naming your sections, try to keep it short and to the point. Although OneNote does not limit the number of characters you can use, titles that are too long will usually prove quite inefficient. You want them to be easily recognizable and jog your memory. Also, big titles can increase the application response time.

Likewise, you can (and should) name your pages and here, too, you should stick to the "more is less" routine.

Creating new sections in a notebook is very simple and doesn't require you to make any choices, as there are no templates for the sections. There is only one type of section available.

However, you can use different colors to make certain sections stand out, and you can also protect the more sensitive ones with individual passwords.

Creating And Storing Information

There are two main ways to collect and store information in OneNote. The first is via the main program window and the second is using Side Note utility. In addition to this, once you have the application installed on your system, you will have the option to send files directly to OneNote from your web browser.

As explained, the program is suited to handle and store all sorts of data, including images and multimedia. Every page can contain any amount of information, so the only limiting factor in that regard is the ease of access. Overcrowded pages are not easy on the eyes and make browsing for information a rather complicated process.

OneNote makes great use of containers when storing information. Every new piece of information is stored in a separate container, which makes handling, searching, and rearranging your notes as simple as it gets. Unlike other MS Office applications, OneNote does not require you to insert the containers manually and then add content to them. Instead, every time you add a new note, image, or clipping, a new container is created automatically. Once it's placed on the page, you can drag the container (and its contents) around, resize it, or delete it as necessary. You can also manipulate individual objects inside a particular container just as easily.

While your notes will typically mostly contain text, the fact that you are not limited in this regard is really helpful. For example, if you ever need to reference an external file, stored locally, on the network, or anywhere on the Web, you can do this by using the Insert tab. Under this tab, you will find the Link button, which will allow you to point to the desired file. If you want to insert the contents of the file instead, you can do this by selecting File Printout and then locate the file you want.

For those who enjoy handwritten notes, there is a pen tool, which can be controlled using the mouse. Tablet users can insert handwritten notes using the tablet pen.

Additional Formatting

For better organization and clarity of your notes, there are additional formatting options you can utilize. When it comes to text, there are all standard options that you are used to if you've used MS Office programs like Word. You can pick the alignment within the container, determine spacing between the lines, and create different types of lists (numbered, bulleted, etc.)

Paragraphs can be assigned different levels (total of five), and these levels will be distinguished by the indentation from the left margin. To create the indent, simply place the cursor at the start of a desired paragraph and press Tab once or several times, depending on the level you want to designate.

This can be very useful later on because you can simply select all paragraphs at a certain level. Simply right-click the header of the container you want to edit, pick Select from the drop-down menu, and designate the desired level (All at Level 1, All at Level 2, etc.)

In addition to adding paragraph levels, you can also further distinguish different types of notes by changing the backgrounds for certain sections and pages. By default, all new sections in OneNote have a plain, white background.

For particular pages, you can right-click the page tab and move your mouse to the Section Color item in the drop-down menu. From there, you can pick any color you like for the particular page.

Tagging

To further simplify going through your notes, OneNote offers a neat little option to "tag" the content. Tags are simple visual identifiers, small icons basically, that you attach to different notes to make them easier to locate later.

There are almost thirty tags that come readily available in OneNote for you to use, but if this is not enough, you can also create your own. Some of the tags delivered with the application include Idea, Movie to See, Contact, Phone number, Password, To Do tags, Critical, etc.

You can simply attach a tag to any paragraph you want by right-clicking inside it and then select the appropriate tag. It will be attached to the content, and you will be able to locate it later by filtering the appropriate tag.

Collecting Outside Information

One of the more convenient functions of the OneNote is its flexibility and simplicity when handling outside information. Content from any screen can be sent to one note as a screen clipping in a matter of seconds. Likewise, you can send entire web pages to the program, in the form of web notes.

You can adjust options inside the application so to always know what exactly to do when outside information is sent to it. With web notes, there are four possibilities:

– - OneNote can always ask you where you want to send this new information,

– - You can set it up so to always send it to the current page,

– - You can also always send new data to a new page, or

– - You can set a default location where all web notes will be stored automatically.

For screen clippings, there are three available options:

- – - Always ask when the information is sent,

- – - Store the clipping to the Clipboard, and you can then paste it wherever you want

- – - Set a default location to which all screen clippings are sent automatically.

You can capture screen clippings using the OneNote tool designed for this particular purpose. It is located under the Insert tab of the software. Once you click the Screen Clipping button, OneNote will minimize to the taskbar, allowing you to capture the entire screen or a relevant portion of the screen.

As for web notes, if you are using Internet Explorer, you can send any web page to OneNote by using the Explorer's Tools menu. There will be an item Send to OneNote there, and by clicking it you will get a dialogue asking you where you want to send information to, or it will be sent to the predetermined location.

Creating Video And Audio Notes

Finally, if the text and static pictures are just not doing it for you, you can also make audio and video notes just as easily. If you are using a PC or a laptop, you will need a microphone to record audio and a camera for video. All phones and tablets already have a microphone, and most of them also have a camera, so mobile users can really take a full advantage of this option without any additional hassle.

In addition to being able to record and store your notes, the software also gives you the option to enable the search using the spoken words. That way, even if you have a lot of voice notes stored in your notebook, you will be able to search through them easily. Of course, for this function to work properly, the audio must be of high quality and the words need to be pronounced clearly. There are several languages supported for this function besides English, including German, Italian, French, Japanese, and even Traditional Chinese.

Using Side Note

You don't have to have the OneNote application running at all times to be able to take quick notes. You can also use Side Note, which is a basic, light version of the full software.

You can quickly access the simplified Side Note interface by clicking the OneNote icon in the notification area of the Windows Taskbar. This light interface will give you all the quick options readily available to make any quick notes and get on with your business.

Chapter 4
OneNote In Your Everyday Life

Now that you understand what OneNote is, and you have an overview of its numerous functionalities, you could still be wondering, why do I need it? No doubt, all these possibilities sound great on paper, but what is that OneNote can do for you to actually make your life better? After all, any software worth your time must offer something that will make your life, private or professional, simpler, save you time, or help you deliver a better product. So, where does OneNote fit in?

At a first glance, it may seem that this application does not offer anything revolutionary and that other programs already have all of this (and more). To an extent, this is true, but what makes OneNote stand out is the fact it combines all of these capabilities in one place and, even more importantly, makes them all cooperate and work together.

Let us start with a very simple example of a grocery list. You have a notebook with different sections covering your private life, and one of them is grocery shopping. You are about to start preparing a Sunday meal, so you update the grocery list and send your kid (or husband, when it comes to grocery shopping, there isn't that much difference) to fetch what you need.

Five minutes later, you realize you've forgotten about a few items that you need. Now, you could call to let them know and keep your fingers crossed that it doesn't slip their mind by the time they reach the cashier. Or, you can simply open the list in OneNote and add the items. Once they open it on their phones, it will automatically update, and there will be no need for them to remember anything. It will all be there.

This may sound like a rather simple example, but it is one that we can all relate to (regardless of whether you are the one making the list or the one doing the shopping). Nobody likes waiting time, and everybody hates making another trip to the store just to buy some more milk and a dozen eggs. This way, everybody's happy, and everybody gets what they want.

Professionals who conduct a lot of interviews will also find OneNote very handy. You can prepare all your questions inside the app and then use the same app to record the interview as you read the questions and make any additional notes as you go. You will end up with a lot of useful information in one place, and the transcribing will be much easier. You could even have the audio turned into text using voice recognition and then just edit any errors or inconsistencies.

If you keep track of your spending (like all serious adults do, right?), OneNote can be a very handy tool. You can scan or photograph your receipts, and they will automatically have the date and time attached to them. Write down a quick note making a reference to the place and you will have all the necessary info. If at any later point, you need to find the information, the search will be painless. This is particularly useful for people who keep the receipts so they could claim the refunds and similar. All in one place, easily searchable and neatly arranged, courtesy of OneNote.

Properly Using Tags

As explained, tags are very useful tools for organizing your notes in a good fashion. Used correctly, they will make your life much easier. However, don't overuse them and attach a bunch of tags to a single entry, because it will severely decrease its usefulness.

Let us start again with something very simple and relatable. How many times have you seen a trailer for a new movie and thought to yourself, "I need to see this?" The problem is, we usually just make a mental note, thinking that there is no way to forget about such an excellent movie. In reality, it will be gone from your head within a couple of hours and you may or may not remember it at some later point.

Using OneNote, you can just send the entire web page to the designated section of your notebook, tag it with "Movie to See," and forget about it for now. The next time you are bored, you can simply search for this particular tag and see what new movies have caught your attention. From that list, you can then figure out which of those movies are now available in theaters or as video on demand, etc.

A very similar scenario applies to our ideas. Every now and then, you come across a great idea, but it is usually gone as quickly as it has appeared. Unless you write it down somewhere, the odds are, it will be lost forever. And even if you do make a note, if it is stored in some random place, you will likely forget not only about the idea but about the place altogether.

With OneNote, you can make a quick remark, tag it "Idea," and not worry about it. Every now and then you can go through those thoughts tagged "Idea" and see if there is anything worth devoting more time to. I am not saying that you will come up with the next Facebook, but having your thoughts well organized might produce some outstanding results that would have otherwise been lost in the memory limbo, covered with the common, everyday stuff that keeps piling on.

Once you get used to OneNote tagging system, you will simply love it. It is very intuitive and makes a lot of sense, so the more you use the application, the more you will develop your own tagging style and after a while, you will have a lot of useful notes arranged in such a way that you will only need a few clicks to retrieve them.

Using OneNote for Big Projects

While OneNote is clearly very useful for keeping and maintaining your private notes, its capabilities reach far beyond that. This application can also be a very powerful tool for collaboration on big professional projects.

We've already looked into some of the technical aspects regarding sharing the notebooks so I won't spend more time explaining these points. The options are pretty straightforward and simple to use, so you shouldn't have any problems figuring it out.

What really deserves some more attention is the multi-functionality of OneNote. The ability to work with all sorts of files and even copy entire web pages with a single click makes this program an excellent choice for a group of people working together on a big and demanding project.

There are other programs for this particular purpose out there, and some of them do a great job. Nobody can deny this. However, many of these programs are quite restrictive in nature and require users to follow certain rules and to fit their thought processes and ideas within the program's framework.

OneNote, on the other hand, gives users full freedom of expression, from simple textual notes to recording video files. Some people prefer putting their ideas in writing; others are more comfortable with recording their voice while the third may best express themselves through drawings and diagrams.

Regardless of what group you belong to, OneNote can meet your needs. There is no doubt that things can get a bit hectic at times if your team consists of a lot of people with their personal styles. But this can be handled by setting up some organizational rules that everyone needs to follow.

On the other hand, you can be quite confident that you will get the best from everyone. Everybody involve will be free to use the mode of expression they are the most comfortable with and, in most cases, this will result in increased productivity, better ideas, and overall a better mood in the group.

At a first glance, this software may not seem capable of handling big tasks, but in this case, the appearance is deceiving. OneNote hides a lot of power under its somewhat plain looks. The simplicity of the application does not reflect its programming, at least not in a negative way. On the contrary, the plainness is for the user benefit, to make sure you are not overwhelmed. The user interface is friendly and easy to navigate, but that does not mean that the engine behind the software is not a powerful one. The box may seem simple, but what's inside it is most certainly not.

OneNote for Students

Students are one group that was apparently considered when the OneNote application was first created. This can be concluded from a number of templates revolving around academic work.

The truth is, OneNote can literally make your life as a student much easier. Taking notes during lectures is a common practice, but very often it is hard to keep track of everything you write down and, after a while, your handwritten notes can turn into a bit of a mess. Sometimes a good solution is to have a number of different physical notebooks for different lectures, but then you have to remember to take particular notebooks on certain days. Moreover, if you happen to lose one of the notebooks, you could end up losing month's worth of carefully collected notes.

OneNote makes all these problems disappear at once. First of all, you can use your laptop or tablet to write down the notes, which means everything will be readable. We all know too well how painful it can be trying to decipher something you know is important, but you just can't figure out what exactly a certain note says.

The organization is no longer an issue. Since you can have as many notebooks, sections, and pages as you like, you can devise a system that you find easy to work with. All those useful tools that were mentioned, like tags and paragraph levels, are at your disposal to really make your notes into a valuable learning resource.

Losing your notes is also no longer a concern. Even if you happen to lose the laptop or tablet (which is bad enough on its own), you will still have all of your notes. You just need to make sure to store them online, on a service like OneDrive, and even if you misplace one of your devices, the information is still available to you. OneDrive is free to use, fully compatible with OneNote, and offers 15 GB of storage space, which should be plenty. There are free and paid ways to increase the storage as well, should you run low.

Outside of lectures, OneNote can really help you prepare materials for your papers or study for your exams. Since you can fully interact with outside sources and your own notes, it is very easy to move the things around and copy them to a new location. So, for example, you can create a new section for your upcoming paper and fill it with useful notes from the lectures and other information you manage do dig up, like relevant websites, any images or recordings dealing with your topic, etc. Another very useful tidbit is that OneNote will automatically add the source of the content whenever you copy and paste something from the web, saving you some valuable time on creating the bibliography for scientific papers.

A life of a student is complicated enough as it is, so anything that can help you simplify and organize your academic efforts is highly useful. With OneNote, you will get all the solutions you need, gathered in a simple, yet highly functional package.

Additional Applications To Use With OneNote

To make your OneNote experience even better, you can use some of the external add-ons which add or enhance certain functionalities of the program.

Onetastic is a completely free add-on for Microsoft OneNote, being developed by one of the members of the OneNote programming team. Since it is impossible to include every functionality that is out there in the original program, he took it upon himself to develop this cool add-on, which gives you a whole range of new, useful tools.

For example, Onetastic comes with a standalone calendar, which gives you an insight into your notes by dates. You can list the pages by the date they were created or using the time of the last modifications. This comes in handy when you just can't remember the right keyword to search for but have an idea about when you created a particular note that you want to retrieve.

This add-on will also give you a possibility to add custom styles to OneNote. While this is a mostly cosmetic option, it is still a nice feature to have, especially since it comes free of charge.

OneNote has a pretty good inbuilt OCR (Optical Character Recognition) engine, which makes it possible to copy the text from any image and move it to Word or any other text processing software. However, it lacks the ability to only select parts of the text from an image. With Onetastic, you will also be able to do this, which comes in handy when you only want to extract a partial text and not have to deal with the rest.

Finally, Onetastic also comes with a macro processor and editor, enabling you to create macros for common tasks. Once you make a macro, these tasks will become as simple as clicking a single button. A lot of macros are readily delivered with the add-on, but you are completely free to create your own.

Onetastic is the brainchild of Omer Atay, and it is fully supported and recommended by the MS Office team.

Office Lens is another great add-on for OneNote. With it, you can take a picture of a whiteboard or a document and have it move instantly to OneNote. The add-on can even turn these photos into editable MS Word documents. Unlike Onetastic, which is unfortunately only available for desktop computers and laptops at the time, this add-on can be downloaded for all types of phones and tablets.

There are also several add-ons which can turn your OneNote into a news reader, bringing the news from your favorite sources directly into the app, without you having to browse through the sites.

Final OneNote Tips And Tricks

All these capabilities and functionalities of OneNote, combined with external add-ons, can clearly help you achieve so much more with far less effort. That said, the key to extracting the maximum out of OneNote is organization.

At the end of the day, for most users OneNote will be a highly personal application. This means that you will want to adjust it for your particular needs and, even more importantly, synchronize it in a manner that fits the way you think and work.

It may sound easier than it actually is. The reality is, what is a great organization for one user can seem like an undecipherable mess for another. You want to make your OneNote really work for you.

The best way to tackle this issue is by simply starting to take notes. Perhaps you'd like to create a structure first, but if you haven't used the software before, it will be very hard for you to have a good idea of what exactly to expect. Instead, spend some time taking useful notes (for whatever purpose you need them), perhaps tagging them as you go, and let some content build up.

After a couple of weeks (it could be more, it could be less, depending on how frequently you take the notes), take a few hours to go through all of your notes and see what they look like. What is in there? How often do you type in the stuff yourself? How often do you import things from the web?

By this point, you should have a clear picture about the way you like to take your notes and what type of content prevails in them. You can then proceed to build the structure that best fits your note taking habits. Once you create the structure, you can keep using it for new entries, and you will see how things nicely fall in place.

If you need to keep your personal and professional notes separate, you can always create multiple folders. That way notes from completely different areas of your life will never cross paths, and the information will be much easier to browse through. This is not obligatory at any rate, but it can be helpful if you have a lot of information from different areas.

You can even create new folders for brand new and important projects. Once you are done with them, you may want to remove them from your computer or tablet, since local copies can take a lot of space after a while. Simply burn them to a CD or move them to another hard drive you use for backups and archives and move on. If you ever need the old project again, it will be easily retrievable.

Chapter 5
Staying Organized With Onenote

Understanding what you can do with OneNote might be exciting to learn, but don't run off to use this application just yet. When using any organizational tool – whether manual or otherwise – it's always easier to get disorganized than to stay organized when you don't work smartly. In fact, most of us start out using various exciting tools only to forget and break from our good routines within a week or so. How many times have you started a profound journey towards a more efficient life only to fail by a moon's turn, if not sooner? If you want to make a notable change, OneNote makes things easier, but there are several conscious decisions you need to make for yourself.

We all have our own organizational methods, and to each his own is certainly valid here. You don't need to use methods which you're not comfortable with or ones that aren't effective for you. In fact, a blogger or CEO can both use OneNote to better their lives, but the way they use the tool will differ – even if just by a bit. However, before we tweak our tools for our requirements, we need to be in the habit of using them. If you're constantly finding yourself in a disorganized position, it's time to understand and correct the heart of the problem. Most people are hindered by six common and solvable roadblocks on their path to productivity.

Problem: You don't know how to organize

Organizing your life is a skill. It's honed through practice and learning, but you do need a strong base to stand from. Simply using OneNote won't make you magically productive, but it can help considerably.

For example, we've talked about tags in the earlier chapters. When used effectively, they're a powerful tool. When used for the heck of it, you're likely going to find yourself in a disorganized position in no time. We've discussed how tags can be used for maximizing efficiency, and much of the same principles can be used for practicing organization. You eliminate items you don't need, categorize every other item into their related class and then organize each group into functional forms, and repeat.

Problem: You're overwhelmed

Taking the first step is always the hardest part. After all, you might not exactly know what direction to take a step in. Cutting tasks into sub-tasks is an effective way of getting started. Simplify the equation for yourself and break everything down into smaller tasks. OneNote, with its pages and sections, is great for breaking things down. Spend fifteen minutes at night developing small goals to achieve your overall daily objectives.

Problem: You can't find time to organize yourself

Between life, work and other activities, it's easy to forget tasks which we're not used to. To use OneNote, you need to get in the habit of using it. Allocate a time to start the app up and organize yourself. There's no trick to it; it's just an effort you need to make yourself.

Getting the above three mentioned aspects in order will help you develop a habit of using OneNote. That being said, staying organized requires good practices. Many times, we find ourselves cleaning our messes, only for them to return two weeks later. With good practices, however, you'll be able to make sure everything is as tidy as you need it to be.

Now let's start out by discussing how you can ensure you're always organized while using OneNote. First things first: Create as many notebooks you need, not one more or one less. As discussed earlier, OneNote is broken down into notebooks, sections, and pages. Each tool has its own purpose, and each is an active member in determining clutter. While providing team or private notebooks, OneNote does not provide password protected sections or pages, so making multiple notebooks is fairly common. Having more notebooks, however, doesn't necessarily mean you will be more efficient. In fact, you can end up hindering the efficiency you could have. Most individuals find 2-3 Notebooks efficient enough for daily or team working.

Now when it comes to naming each aspect, be precise. The beauty of OneNote is how easy things can be made or found, but you do need to make an initial effort. Say you want to develop an employee payroll in your Employee Notebook. Instead of leaving each section with a generic name, use a price title for your section. It'll save you more time when scanning for your employee payroll, avoid confusion and allow you to make fewer mistakes. Likewise, each employee can have their own page if long term work is a part of the job description. Your goal should be to keep things as neat and tidy as possible – while still being functional.

However, the above is a good practice which can only cause problems later on if you're negligent about it. There are more immediate reasons we might end up with a cluttered mess, and tackling them is crucial. Let's take a look at some formatting tips for OneNote; that can help save you time.

1. **Paragraph where possible** – A common mistake made by many is improper paragraphs. As a rule of thumb, most paragraphs should not exceed 3-4 lines, and sentences should be kept short. The less your work looks like an uncontrollable ramble, the more likely you are to keep your notebook clutter-free.

2. **Make use of headings and subheadings** – Setting up a hierarchy can really make a difference. When you break down information, you're increasing readability and search

ability of your documents. This will make your text more structured and less messy.

3. **Don't forget about font colors and highlighters** – You might not want to go overboard with this tool, but font colors can be an effective way of color-coding text. If you're working with a team, colors can be used to distinguish everything from additions or comments. Likewise, highlighters can be used to spotlight important text.

4. **Bold and italics can be pretty handy as well** – If you're looking to make a certain word, line or paragraph stand out, using bold and italics can really help. You can also subscript or strikethrough words as well.

5. **Lists and bullet points** – Do you have a bunch of points which can be grouped together? Using lists or bullet points help clear up this potential clutter. Just remember, if items need to appear with some order, use numbered lists. Otherwise, bullet points will do the trick.

6. **Need a guide? Use lines** – By default, OneNote presents us with a blank page. Some people find having a lined background is less cluttered and more manageable. If you're one of them, you can simply add in your preferred background. Right-click on your page to toggle between having a blank page or a lined page. Alternatively, you can also add in graphs or ruled paper, depending on your needs. Best of all, you can customize each page to look and feel exactly as you want it.

Does all of this sound simplistic? Give each of these items a try and see the difference they make for you. Develop a habit of using each tool in appropriate situations and it's unlikely you'll ever have a messy day.

Formatting is not the only way to organize your OneNote and save time. This application was designed for business and personal use, and has many pre-built resources you can use to save time.

Being a Microsoft program, you'll find many aspects of OneNote to be already integrated with other Microsoft services. For example, say you wish to make notes for a particular meeting you have. You could create those minutes by manually typing out the details on a page, or you can use the built-in tools to help you. By selecting the Meeting Details option in OneNote, you can access your Microsoft Exchange Calendar via Outlook. Simply select the meeting you wish to make notes on and you'll be provided with a fully formatted page. You will have your meeting's exact title with its date and a list of details such as time of the meeting, location, who is attending and a clean notes section you might wish to add additional information. Using this method, you'll have a standardized way to keep track of what goes on in your meetings, and it'll save you valuable time by arranging everything for you even before you get started.

Now another great option is Email Page. You could have all your employees tracking your meeting conclusion or just one. One person could note all the discussion down and email it to the rest. Email Page would automatically add the entire page to your Outlook email, in addition to email addresses of everyone present at the meeting and a subject for it. All you need to do is press send.

This might be all you need in most cases, however, if you like to get into greater detail, there are more options available for you. OneNote comes with several template options you can access freely. Simply visit the Insert tab and click on Page templates. A list of various templates for different situations will pop up on the right. The best part of templates is that you can build and save your own. If you're working for a company, you can add in the company logo or other information, so when sending out meeting minutes or other notes, you'll have a consistent, professional format.

OneNote also integrates PDFs really well. Any text-format PDF can be easily transferred into the application, but the magic lies in the options it provides. All PDFs are searchable. Say you wish to find a particular chapter in a PDF file. You don't need to open another software or even open the PDF section in OneNote. Just type in the chapter name and you'll be taken there. Now you can highlight, note or comment on that section as you please.

One of the easiest, yet often forgotten techniques to save time are keyboard shortcuts. Aside from the basic copy-paste duo, most of us don't bother taking a look at shortcuts. However, with OneNote, learning shortcuts can be pretty handy. We'll provide you a glossary of keyboard shortcuts at the end of the book for both Windows and Mac users. Look at them often while working until using these easy keys becomes second nature.

Being a powerful, all-purpose program, OneNote even has the ability to add and calculate math equations into your pages. You don't need an extra calculator to solve simple math problems. Simply jot down equations during your meetings or classes and let OneNote do its magic for you. Calculating results takes less time than finding a calculator and fiddling with it. It is also helpful for those who are not quick with math equations or have a hard time remembering the step to solving an equation.

For example, you might want to calculate the sum of 112, 219 and 124. To process the equation, simply type 112+219+124, followed by an equal sign, without any spaces, and then press the spacebar to reveal the answer after the equal sign. Using this method, you can calculate everything from Sin to the square root of any number. There are some operators that need to be used for some functions. For example, to find out the square root, you need to use sqrt and place your subject in brackets before placing your equal sign. You can use this to calculate monthly sales, employee or other expenses, or payments. For students, this provides them with their one-stop notebook for everything. Calculating everything from simple math equations to accounting is made easier with this method. Like shortcuts, we'll add a glossary of terms which can be calculated through OneNote.

Chapter 6
Troubleshooting Synchronization Errors
In Onenote 2016 For Windows

Part of time management is ensuring your work goes smoothly and efficiently. Like with clutter, if you're not careful, you might end up messing something up, which means more wasted time. However, some problems are inevitable.

Even though OneNote is designed to be seamless by constantly syncing with servers, it's possible an error might cause trouble with syncing. So your time isn't wasted, let's discuss a few ways you can ensure this issue is resolved as quickly as possible.

Start by resetting a notebook that won't sync. If your notebook can't seem to back up on OneDrive or SharePoint, try opening the web version. If OneNote Online is syncing with itself, you can determine whether the problem is occurring through OneNote itself or a different program. If it isn't, then Microsoft servers might be having an issue.

How to open OneNote Online?

Open OneNote on your device and go to File, then Info. Copy the URL shown below the problem notebook and paste it into the address box of your web browser, then press Enter to load the notebook in OneNote Online.

If you've reached this point, and servers are functioning properly, then the issue lies within your desktop version instead. Now you can start resetting the notebook by going into File, then Info. Make sure you don't close the web version during this process. Locate your affected notebook and go into its settings to close the notebook. Switch to your notebook in OneNote Online and select the Open in OneNote option. This should solve the issue for you. If, however, the problem isn't resolved, you can contact Microsoft services. Their official support is fast and will solve your issue in no time at all.

Notebook Syncs aren't the only problems that might occur. Sometimes a section within a shared notebook may be compromised. This bad section will be due to improper sync on your shared network. Start by opening OneNote and choose File, Info and View Sync Status. A dialog box showing Shared Notebook Synchronization should open up. If any of your notebooks have a yellow triangle warning next its name, a portion of that notebook might be causing sync problems. Choose the Sync Now option next to the notebook's name. If this problem keeps repeating, simply create a new section in the same notebook and copy all the information from your troubled section to the new one you've just created. However, copy but don't move. Moving might transfer whatever problem the old section has into the new section. After that, just press shift+F9 to sync your section and notebook manually. You can now delete the old section. Repeat check when you're done to ensure the problem has been fixed.

Likewise, it's equally important to ensure you always have a backup on hand. OneNote saves notes automatically as you work, but backing up your notebook is just that extra safety measure you need to ensure data stays where you want it to. Hard drive crashes can happen to anyone at any time, and like your other files, information within OneNote can be compromised as well. If there is no backup, your notes will be gone forever. By backing up your notebooks, you'll be able to restore your notes if such an unfortunate incident occurs.

A built-in aspect of backing up is that automatic backups can be set after you choose a location where you want to store your files. You might have a backup on your computer's hard drive, but the entire point of this backup is to store your files on a device which can be used to restore data if something malfunctions on your hard drive. So, make sure you don't pick a location on your computer for this particular backup. If you are working for a company, you could use a company server or other cloud/backup services for this function.

To start backing up, choose File and go into Options. In the dialogue box, locate and choose Save & Backup. On the right, you should see a Backup Folder under the Save heading and then select Modify. Now you can choose the folder you wish to back up your notebook into. You can use servers, private folders or even USB drives. Remember to click OK when you're done. By default, OneNote is programmed to automatically update your backup each week. However, you can change the frequency of backups if you happen to take a lot of important notes. Save & Backup settings should provide you with everything you need to back up your data however frequently you want to.

If you are between scheduled backups and you jotted down some important notes, OneNote gives you the option to manually backup your notes. Simply enter File and Options. Choose Save & Backup options and select Backup All Notebooks Now under the Save option on the right. When all notebooks are backed up, click OK to close.

You might not necessarily want to override your previous backups in some cases. IF such a case occurs, you can set OneNote to use numbered backups to store all of the copies that you need. There may be instances that down the road you need to reference something that you had put into OneNote and then deleted when you thought you were finished with it. By numbering your back ups these will still be saved. It just may take some time to go through them to find what you are looking for.

Even if you're not setting a backup schedule, all is not lost in case you can't find some notes. OneNote keeps a few automatic backups by default, but you will need to figure out where your application stores information. Some devices may actually store information on OneDrive. You may search for backups by going into File, Info and Open Backups. If your notes are saved on OneDrive, you will need to visit the Recycle Bin to recover information.

There might be cases where you need to change the permissions of a certain notebook. It could be new entrants or exits from currently shared notebooks, or you want to close a notebook at the end of a project.

If your notebook is on OneDrive, you can change the permission for individuals who can view or edit files. Simply go to File, Share and Share with People to adjust the permissions. You'll need to right-click the person's name you wish to give or revoke permission from and choose the appropriate option. Select Can Edit if you would like someone to be able to edit and make changes to the selected notebook. Select Can View if you simply wish for them to be able to open it without editing the contents.

Sometimes, however, you may want to revoke any kind of access from a user. In that case, choose the Remove User option and that person won't have any further access to your notebook. If you don't see anyone listed in this section, you're not sharing that notebook with anyone currently.

This isn't applicable to a shared link. If you have shared a notebook using a shareable link, you will need to stop that link from working. Otherwise, individuals can use that link to view or edit your notebook. To stop a link from working, click File, Share and Get a Sharing Link. You'll see three options, View Link, Edit Link or Disable Link. Select the last one to disable it from further viewing. Individuals who try to access your notebook through a disabled link will get a message telling them their selected link might be deleted or expired, or they may not have permission to view it.

If you can't see a link, then you are not sharing your notebook with anyone. Now, you don't necessarily need to share an entire notebook to share ideas. You can export any OneNote page as a PDF or send it in an email to others. In some cases, to avoid clutter, you might want to delete your notebook entirely – that is, if you're done with it yourself.

Lastly, you might consider password protecting your notes. If you're concerned about keeping your thoughts or work private and away from prying eyes, password protection is a built-in feature. You can't password protect a whole notebook, but you can change them from private to shared. Sections, however, can be password-protected. When a section is protected by a password, all of its pages are locked until the correct password is provided to the prompt.

To add protection to a certain section, right-click it and then choose Password Protect this Section. A task panel should open up in front of you. Select Set Password and enter the password you want in the password protection dialog box. You'll need to confirm the password by retyping it and hitting the OK button when you're done. Always remember to choose your password carefully and be extra wary of what you type since passwords are case sensitive. If you forget it, no one will be able to unlock it for you. There is no support for such recovery since passwords are saved only on your local computer. Once it's gone, it's gone. If you're working in a group, make sure everyone else has or is able to remember the password as well.

Locking a protected section in your notebook needs to be done manually. Luckily, there is a way you can lock all of your password protected sections in one step. Right click any of your protected, currently unlocked section tabs, and then select Password Protect this Section. Once the password protection task panel springs up, select Lock All to secure all of them.

While you can't access forgotten passwords, you can change a password if needed. Right-click the section tab that has the password you wish to change and choose Password Protect this Section. In the task panel, select Change Password. If you don't see this option is not yet available to you, or a password has not been applied to that section yet. Now, type in the current password in the provided old password section. Then type in your new password and confirm it again before pressing OK.

Removing a password from a protected section is easy as well. You just need to right-click the tab you wish to remove your password from, select the Password Protect this Section option and choose Remove Password. Again, if you see nothing in this area, your password wasn't applied. You'll need to type in your current password to verify the removal and click okay to make your section accessible.

OneNote, being the versatile app it is, provides you with options to customize the way password protection works. By default, password protected sections are locked automatically if you're not actively working on them. You can, however, curate the time period and other details of how password protection is applied to any particular section.

Start by going into File and Options. Next, you'll want to dive into the Advanced section and find Passwords.

You'll be presented with a few options. You can lock your notebook section after a specified amount of time according to your preference. You can immediately lock a section when you navigate away from a particular section, or you can make notes in password protected areas temporarily available to other programs, such as add-ins, to access password protected sections when they are unlocked only. Choose the one that matches your preference and hit OK.

You won't be able to access protected information through notebook searches until they are unlocked first. Likewise, any tags appearing in password protected sections are not going to be included in a note tag summary until the section is unlocked.

You should now be able to solve common issues which may arise from using OneNote and avoid any wasted time which can hamper your productivity. If, however, you are unable to resolve your issues, contact Microsoft Office's help to get further assistance.

Chapter 7
Applying What You've Learned So Far

We've covered a lot over the past few chapters, and it may seem overwhelming to take in all at once. Let's take a breather and learn by checking out a few examples. After all, the best way to learn the extent of OneNote's power and use is by example. So in this section, we'll take a look at different ways you can apply things you've learned so far about OneNote.

Let's start by using a math class as an example. Math is a daunting subject that can easily end up as a clutter since it deals with so many different aspects. You have numbers mixed in with words, graphs, charts...You name it. Problems are sometimes worded to be confusing. Teaching math is often as frustrating for teachers to teach as much as learning it is for students. One of the reasons math is so difficult to learn is due to the way it's taught. Most research in recent years suggests how traditional teaching methods aren't optimal. Students simply don't learn through simple whiteboard teaching, since it's not interactive. All you need to do is make your Math class more interactive. However, when you try to incorporate math with technology, things will seem more difficult than they already are. For one, math still requires students to learn by hand. When they formulate or solve equations through written means, they're more like to remember concepts taught to them. Many software programs aren't able to provide the kind of atmosphere students and teachers need to provide any positive results when teaching with technology. That is, many aside from OneNote. OneNote is the perfect tool to integrate both written and interactive learning, and streamline the entire process. You just need to be creative.

So, how can you turn this software into a digital schoolbag to teach math?

Start out by creating a shared notebook for your class. Share it with students and name each section with all the topics you need to cover for that year. You can either have pre-built notes, use OneNote to present a lecture using a projector and a stylus, or do both. It's up to you and your pupils as to how you might want to use this method. This makes it easy to keep track of what you're teaching and increases access to your class notes. Students will be able to go back and see exactly what you've taught and what concepts you have used.

Your lessons can be made more interactive through properly illustrated diagrams or animations. Sometimes simply having visually appealing content is enough for some students to become more attentive and engrossed in the lecture. There are also students that learn more effectively by visualization. So to use visual graphics to explain the lessons can be a huge benefit to the students' academic progress.

Likewise, you can even have a notebook for student or group assignments. Students can learn with each other from the methodologies each student uses and be teachers for their peers as well. Likewise, you can provide can another Notebook where your students can provide you feedback or ask questions. This will ensure all students are on the same page. Schedules for test days and even reminders can be sent out to students, so they're always informed.

If you're sharing some theories which require reading, you can make the student's job easier or at least ask students to highlight important paragraphs and lines to see how much they've learned through that reading.

The best part is the ability to be creative. Using web-integrations and add-ins, you can make your class a more fun place to learn. For example, students can be asked to calculate the area of a real life location and take pictures of the location to make things more interesting for them. If your students don't have tablets, they can use pictures to submit their assignments or work as well.

OneNote can be an excellent tool for teachers since it helps increase student engagement and keeps track of what happens in each class. Teachers can take a look at their own work or their student's work when developing classes for future students, and learn from their own positives and negatives as well.

Next, let's look at how bloggers can make use of OneNote. In this day and age, capturing a reader's attention requires more than just good content, and you need to make things entertaining and exciting for the reader. One such method is to make your content visually appealing. Clean layouts and organized pages attract readers, so it's crucial for bloggers to have visual content. While providing all the basic features word processors provide, OneNote goes a bit further and is able to help bloggers design their blogs. They can set up a template to look like their website or blog, and write in content to see how it looks before they post it on their website.

Bloggers can even have a notebook for storing information for future pieces or projects, save voice memos or embed video ideas. They can even clip information from the internet to read for later use. PDFs can be placed with important points highlighted for later use. Since you can use phrases to find materials in a PDF through OneNote, bloggers will have a powerful reading tool in their arsenal.

Scheduling is perhaps the biggest issue faced by bloggers. Organizing yourself and remembering to post new content, but OneNote is here to help. The benefit of OneNote is how easy it is to set up a schedule. You can use a template or link it up with a Microsoft-based calendar. Reminders can also be set up to consistently churn out work at the right time and keep readers coming back for more.

For managers, this is a much-needed tool that combines a lot of aspects they utilize consistently. They can control everything from their to-do lists to sending out memos to their employees. Having notebooks for multiple items gives them access to managing various projects, personal or otherwise, all in one place. It's a must-try tool to keep you organized and increase your company's productivity.

Chapter 8
OneNote Add-Ins

We briefly touched upon how additional applications can be integrated with OneNote to enrich this powerful software even more. But let's look at some of the best resources you can make use of.

Feedly

One of the top RSS readers available, Feedly, is available to integrate with OneNote. You'll need to be a Feedly Pro user to take advantage of this opportunity, but you'll be glad to do so. Feedly is known for its quick performance, elegant design, and feature-filled functionality. Whether you're doing research or just came across a must-read article, you can save it to OneNote without having to search for it again.

OneNote Clipper

This feature often comes pre-built, but can be downloaded if it's not installed on your device. Clip from the web easily and markup any image with a stylus – a huge help for online and offline purposes.

Office Lens

We've mentioned Office Lens above so we won't dive much into it, but whether you're a student or a working professional, this is a must-have for everyone.

Onetastic for OneNote

Another add-in we can't stop gushing about—with reason. It just gives you limitless power and is definitely worth checking out.

Zapier or IFFFT

Zapier allows you to create a series of "zaps," automated processes to achieve a certain result. Built for businesses, Zapier is the perfect plug-in for OneNote, which extends its use and benefit even more. For example, you can automatically tag certain emails to save in OneNote. Zapier not giving you the automation you need? IFFFT is there to fix that. Both plug-ins operate on the same basis but have different things to offer.

Mind Map for OneNote

Do you use a lot of mind maps? To save time, you can use this integration to standardize your mind maps and create maps chalked with information without appearing cluttered.

Gem for OneNote

Need to increase the tools you have for OneNote? Gem for OneNote will do just that. With just six tabs, you'll get 230+ tools at your disposal and be able to extend what you thought was possible with OneNote.

A word of caution, though – don't start by adding in features for the just f9r the sake of them. Use OneNote and add in things you need in order to make your software more powerful the way you need.

Chapter 9
OneNote Devices Recommendations

As I have explained in the previous chapters, Microsoft OneNote can run on a variety of devices, and it is not limited to Windows-only machines. If you are considering taking this application for a spin but do not have a device that you believe would be suitable, here are a few recommendations. The devices listed here will have no problems supporting all functions of OneNote and will not cost you a small fortune.

Laptops

Acer Aspire E 15 ES1-512-C323 is my top pick in this category. For the price of around $330, you will get everything you need to run OneNote, plus it will also support a number of other everyday operations that you would expect from a quality office laptop.

With a 15.6" screen, it offers plenty of space to work with and a great visibility. It is equipped with 4 GB DDR3L SDRAM, which is really a minimum in this day and age, as you will probably want to run at least Windows 7 as your operating system. It is usually delivered with Windows 8 if that's your cup of tea.

Hard drive with 500 GB of space should prove more than enough for every average personal and professional user, especially concerning OneNote. You want to have plenty of space to go around, simply to be sure.

The only slight drawback of this particular laptop is the Intel Celeron 2.1 Dual-Core processor, but OneNote is not heavy on your processing power anyways. Good amount of RAM is much more important, and this device certainly provides more than enough.

Acer Aspire E 15 comes equipped with WLAN, standard Ethernet port and Bluetooth for the maximum connectivity, which is another important feature for OneNote users. You want to be able to update easily and share your notebooks at all times.

Battery life is decent, capable of withstanding about six - seven hours of operation, which should be plenty for most practical purposes. The keyboard has a nice feel to it and makes typing a pleasant experience. On top of all this, it also comes with an integrated webcam and microphone, which will make creating audio and video entries super simple. The camera is not an HD one, but it will do the job just fine.

Overall, this laptop offers a lot for the money. It is reliable, quiet, and capable of handling a number of tasks simultaneously. You will be able to browse through numerous sources while gathering your OneNote entries without the device freezing on you or overheating.

Asus X551CA is another great laptop for anyone looking for a reliable device for their OneNote needs. At the price of around $260, equipped with 15.6" display and 4 GB DDR3 SDRAM, it will easily return your investment.

Like the Acer, Asus X551CA has a 500 GB hard drive and comes with Windows 8 pre-installed. Without passing judgment, the selection of the operating system is entirely up to you. OneNote will work just fine on any version of the Windows.

This laptop has a better processing power, as it comes equipped with Intel i3 Core processor, so it will naturally run somewhat faster. On the flip side, the battery life of the Asus model is slightly shorter.

This device also comes with the integrated VGA camera and speakers for your video and audio notes. On top of that, it also has a superb sound system and high-quality inbuilt speakers. This extends its use well beyond just OneNote and office work, as it will provide you with a great multimedia experience.

WLAN and Ethernet connections are there, but Bluetooth is missing. This is hardly a big drawback since Bluetooth technology has never really picked up that much. Regardless, it is nice to have full information before making a purchase.

There isn't that much difference between these two overall. If you are looking to buy something with better battery life (if you spend a lot of time traveling, for example), you should probably go for the Acer. On the other hand, if the battery life is not that big of an issue, the Asus will probably give you a bit more in terms of the performance.

If MS OneNote and other applications from the Office package are your primary concern, they will run smoothly on both these models, together with the web browser and background music (if that's your thing), so you shouldn't worry either way.

Tablets

While some users prefer laptops, tablets are clearly becoming a thing of the future. For those who see laptops as the dinosaurs of the past, here are a couple of suggestions for cheap tablets that will handle OneNote just fine.

Lenovo Tab 2 A10 10-Inch. This tablet by Lenovo represents a great mixture of good price and high quality. With 10" display, you will still have a plenty of space to work with while at the same time not having to carry around a relatively heavy laptop.

Lenovo Tab 2 A10 runs on Android, which is not an issue for OneNote users, as an app is readily available in Google Store. It has 2 GB RAM, which may be a little low for laptops, but is just fine for tablets, as you will usually not put them under the same amount of stress.

The processor is the Quad-Core 1.5 GHz MediaTek, which, again, should run most Office-like applications (including OneNote) without any issues. The battery can take about 10 hours of work, and we wouldn't expect anything less from Lenovo, as they've always delivered quality and reliable products.

There are both rear and front cameras as well as one USB port. This port is quite useful, as the tablet comes with only 16 GB of the internal memory. This is quite low, but it can be expanded easily with a really small investment, or you can use external USB drives to store data. On top of that, there are also the online services we mentioned before, so you don't have to store everything locally.

The best part about this tablet is the fact that you can get it for about $180. For everything it offers, this price is really a steal.

Asus Nexus 7-inch is a better fit for those who enjoy a more compact laptop. With only 7" screen, it is highly portable and easy to carry, but it can also be just a bit too small for some users. This boils down to personal preferences.

Asus Nexus comes in two basic variations, one with 16 GB internal memory, and the other one with 32 GB. The former costs around $180, while the latter is a bit more expensive, at around $300.

In terms of the performance, it is very similar to the Lenovo model, as it also has 2 GB RAM and the 1.5 GHz quad-core processor. Nexus also runs on Android.

Thanks to its small size, it is very light, which can certainly be a factor for those who spend a lot of time carrying it around. Despite the size, however, it is a quite powerful little tablet, capable of running OneNote and similar applications without any issues.

Equipped with two cameras (front and back) and high-quality display, it will easily justify the money spent. The battery has a life of about nine hours, which is another big plus.

The only drawback of this laptop is the lack of external storage (no USB ports), and there is no way to expand the memory, so you will have to rely on web storage for bigger files. Still, given how well OneNote works with different Internet services, this should not represent a big problem.

Conclusion

I really hope this book was able to give you a complete picture of OneNote in all of its glory. As you could see, this application is often unjustly neglected, despite being around for a while. Its basic concept may not be anything revolutionary, but the method in which it delivers it certainly is.

It is an application truly created with the end-user and his needs in mind. Instead of restricting and forcing you into limited patterns, it gives you all the freedom to organize your notes any way you see fit and set the things up just the way you like them.

I've tried to list and describe all essential functionalities of the software on these pages. As you start to use it yourself, you will no doubt discover some hidden gems, either on your own or using the endless source of information that is the Internet. Don't be afraid to experiment; always keep in mind that this application's main purpose is to make your life easier, not please anyone else.

The examples and suggestions I mentioned here are only a small part of possible applications for OneNote. There are much, much more. Depending on how creative you are, there is no doubt you will discover some of them as you get used to the software.

In case that you've faced an issue while working with OneNote, simply visit the troubleshooting chapter in this book to get a quick fix so that you can quickly get right back to your organized and efficient life. If you feel limited with the functionality, remember you can always add more features by integrating additional programs.

The final chapter contains some devices that I personally found to be acceptable in terms of both, price and performance, focusing primarily on OneNote functionalities. That said, all of these devices should do just find when facing other similar and everyday tasks. These laptops will not handle the latest games, but will have no problems browsing the Internet, running all types of multimedia, and performing any range of the usual office tasks.

Those who had previous experiences with OneNote will, hopefully, find some useful advice to implement in their everyday routines. As for those who are completely new to this application, I honestly suggest you give it a go for a while and see if it works for you. Most people who try it out get hooked fast, and OneNote becomes a valuable tool in organizing their lives.

Keep in mind that this software comes free of charge, so there is really nothing for you to lose. If you don't like it (which is rarely the case), you can simply forget about it. If you do, however, make sure to tell your friends and give this application some justice. It is a quality piece of software, and it needs to get more on the radar. Don't forget to check out the glossary below to make the most out of your OneNote journey. The vast array of shortcuts is sure to help you become more proficient and organized with OneNote, while taking the hassle out of trying to figure them out for yourself.

Finally, thank you for reading this book. I truly hope it will be a helpful guide on your path of discovering and exploring OneNote. I don't expect you to take my word on the usefulness of this software, but I definitely recommend you to try it out and make up your own mind.

If you received value from this book, then I would like to ask you for a favor. Would you be kind enough to leave a review for this book on Amazon?

Thank you so much!

Glossary: Keyboard Shortcuts – Windows

Keyboard shortcuts require you to press two or more keys in order to activate your command. Keys which need to be pressed simultaneously are separated by a plus (+) sign. That said, there are a few keys which need to be pressed one after the other and those are separated by a comma (,). Let's take a look at all the different combinations you can use in order to save time and be more efficient.

To Do This	Press
Open a new window.	CTRL+M
Open a small window to create a side note.	CTRL+S HIFT+M or Window s+ALT+ N
Dock OneNote window.	CTRL+ALT+D
Undo.	CTRL+Z

Redo.	CTRL+Y
Select all items.	CTRL+A
Cut.	CTRL+X
Copy.	CTRL+C
Paste.	CTRL+V
Move to the start of a line.	HOME
Move to the end of a line.	END
Move left.	LEFT ARROW
Move right.	RIGHT ARROW
Move left by one word.	CTRL+LEFT ARROW
Move right by one word.	CTRL+RIGHT ARROW
Delete left by one character.	BACKSPACE
Delete right by one character.	DELETE
Delete the left by one word.	CTRL+BACKSPACE
Delete right by one character.	CTRL+DELETE
Insert a line	SHIFT+ENTER

break without starting a new paragraph.	
Check spelling.	F7
Open the thesaurus for selected word.	SHIFT+F7
Bring up the context menu for any note, tab, or any other object that currently has focus.	SHIFT+F10
Execute the action suggested on the Information Bar if it appears at the top of a page.	CTRL+SHIFT+W
Highlight selected text.	CTRL+SHIFT+H or CTRL+ALT+H
Insert a link.	CTRL+K
Copy the formatting of selected text (Format Painter).	CTRL+SHIFT+C
Paste the formatting to selected text	CTRL+SHIFT+V

(Format Painter).

Open a link. NOTE: The cursor must be placed anywhere within the formatted link text.	ENTER
Apply or remove bold formatting from the selected text.	CTRL+B
Apply or remove italic formatting from the selected text.	CTRL+I
Apply or remove the underline from the selected text.	CTRL+U
Apply or remove strikethrough from the selected text.	CTRL+HYPHEN
Apply or remove superscript formatting from the selected text.	CTRL+SHIFT+=
Apply or remove	CTRL+=

subscript formatting from the selected text.	
Apply or remove bulleted list formatting from the selected paragraph.	CTRL+PERIOD
Apply or remove numbered list formatting from the selected paragraph.	CTRL+SLASH
Apply a Heading 1 style to the current note.	CTRL+ALT+1
Apply a Heading 2 style to the current note.	CTRL+ALT+2
Apply a Heading 3 style to the current note.	CTRL+ALT+3
Apply a Heading 4 style to the current note.	CTRL+ALT+4
Apply a Heading 5 style to the current note.	CTRL+ALT+5

Apply a Heading 6 style to the current note.	CTRL+ALT+6
Apply the Normal style to the current note.	CTRL+SHIFT+N
Indent a paragraph from the left.	ALT+SHIFT+RIGHT ARROW
Remove a paragraph indent from the left.	ALT+SHIFT+LEFT ARROW
Right-align the selected paragraph.	CTRL+R
Left-align the selected paragraph.	CTRL+L
Increase the font size of selected text.	CTRL+SHIFT+>
Decrease the font size of selected text.	CTRL+SHIFT+<
Clear all formatting applied to the selected text.	CTRL+SHIFT+N

Show or hide rule lines on the current page.	CTRL+SHIFT+R
To Do This	Press
Insert a document or file on the current page.	ALT+N, F
Insert a document or file as a printout on the current page.	ALT+N, O
Show or hide document printouts on the current page (when running OneNote in High Contrast mode).	ALT+SHIFT+P
Insert a picture from a file.	ALT+N, P
Insert a picture from a scanner or a camera.	ALT+N, S
Insert a screen clipping. NOTE: The OneNote icon must be active in	Windows logo key+S

the notification area, at the far right of the Windows taskbar.	
Insert the current date.	ALT+SHIFT+D
Insert the current date and time.	ALT+SHIFT+F
Insert the current time.	ALT+SHIFT+T
Insert a line break.	SHIFT+ENTER
Start a math equation or convert selected text to a math equation.	ALT+=
Insert a Euro (€) symbol.	CTRL+ALT+E
Create a table by adding a second column to already typed text.	TAB
Create another column in a table with a single row.	TAB

Create another row when at the end cell of a table. NOTE: Press ENTER a second time to finish the table.	ENTER
Create a row below the current row in a table.	CTRL+ENTER
Create another paragraph in the same cell in a table.	ALT+ENTER
Create a column to the right of the current column in a table.	CTRL+ALT+R
Create a row above the current one in a table (when the cursor is at the beginning of any row).	ENTER
Delete the current empty row in a table (when the cursor is at the beginning of the	DEL (press twice)

row).	
Select all items on the current page. Press CTRL+A more than once to increase the scope of the selection.	CTRL+A
Select to the end of the line.	SHIFT+END
Select the whole line (when the cursor is at the beginning of the line).	SHIFT+DOWN ARROW
Jump to the title of the page and select it.	CTRL+SHIFT+T
Cancel the selected outline or page.	ESC
Move the current paragraph or several selected paragraphs up.	ALT+SHIFT+UP ARROW
Move the current paragraph or several selected paragraphs down.	ALT+SHIFT+DO WN ARROW

Move the current paragraph or several selected paragraphs left (decreasing the indent).	ALT+SHIFT+LEFT ARROW
Move the current paragraph or several selected paragraphs right (increasing the indent).	ALT+SHIFT+RIGHT ARROW
Select the current paragraph and its subordinate paragraphs.	CTRL+SHIFT+HYPHEN
Delete the selected note or object.	DELETE
Move to the beginning of the line.	HOME
Move to the end of the line.	END
Move one character to the left.	LEFT ARROW
Move one character to the	RIGHT ARROW

right.	
Go back to the last page visited.	ALT+LEFT ARROW
Go forward to the next page visited.	ALT+RIGHT ARROW
Start playback of a selected audio or video recording.	CTRL+ALT+P or CTRL+ALT+S
Rewind the current audio or video recording by a few seconds.	CTRL+ALT+Y
Fast-forward the current audio or video recording by a few seconds.	CTRL+ALT+U
Apply, mark, or clear the To Do tag.	CTRL+1
Apply or clear the Important tag.	CTRL+2
Apply or clear the Question tag.	CTRL+3
Apply or clear the Remember for later tag.	CTRL+4
Apply or clear the	CTRL+5

Definition tag.	
Apply or clear a custom tag.	CTRL+6
Apply or clear a custom tag.	CTRL+7
Apply or clear a custom tag.	CTRL+8
Apply or clear a custom tag.	CTRL+9
Set writing direction left to right.	CTRL+LEFT SHIFT
Set writing direction right to left.	CTRL+RIGHT SHIFT
Increase indent by one level in right-to-left text.	TAB
Decrease indent by one level in right-to-left text.	SHIFT+TAB
Enable or disable full page view.	F11
Open a new OneNote window.	CTRL+M
Open a small	CTRL+SHIFT+M

OneNote window to create a side note.	
Expand or collapse the tabs of a page group.	CTRL+SHIFT+*
Print the current page.	CTRL+P
Add a new page at the end of the selected section.	CTRL+N
Increase the width of the page tabs bar.	CTRL+SHIFT+[
Decrease the width of the page tabs bar.	CTRL+SHIFT+]
Create a new page below the current page tab at the same level.	CTRL+ALT+N
Decrease indents of the current page tab label.	CTRL+ALT+[
Increase indents of the current page tab label.	CTRL+ALT+]
Create a new	CTRL+SHIFT+AL

subpage below the current page.	T+N
Select all items. Press CTRL+A several times to increase the scope of the selection.	CTRL+A
Select the current page.	CTRL+SHIFT+A If the selected page is part of a group, press CTRL+A to select all of the pages in the group.
Move the selected page tab up.	ALT+SHIFT+UP ARROW
Move the selected page tab down.	ALT+SHIFT+DO WN ARROW
Move the insertion point to the page title.	CTRL+SHIFT+T
Go to the first page in the currently visible set of page tabs.	ALT+PAGE UP
Go to the last page in the currently visible set of page tabs.	ALT+PAGE DOWN

Scroll up in the current page.	PAGE UP
Scroll down in the current page.	PAGE DOWN
Scroll to the top of the current page.	CTRL+HOME
Scroll to the bottom of the current page.	CTRL+END
Go to the next paragraph.	CTRL+DOWN ARROW
Go to the previous paragraph.	CTRL+UP ARROW
Go to the next note container.	ALT+DOWN ARROW
Go to the beginning of the line.	HOME
Go to the end of the line.	END
Move one character to the left.	LEFT ARROW
Move one character to the right.	RIGHT ARROW
Go back to the	ALT+LEFT

last page visited.	ARROW
Go forward to the next page visited.	ALT+RIGHT ARROW
Zoom in.	ALT+CTRL+PLU S SIGN (on the numeric keypad) or ALT+CTRL+SHIF T+PLUS SIGN
Zoom out.	ALT+CTRL+MIN US SIGN (on the numeric keypad) or ALT+CTRL+SHIF T+HYPHEN
Save changes.	CTRL+S
Open OneNote.	Windows logo key+SHIFT+N
Open a notebook.	CTRL+O
Send to OneNote Tool	Windows logo key+N
Create a new section.	CTRL+T
Open a section.	CTRL+ALT+SHIF T+O
Go to the next section.	CTRL+TAB

Go to the previous section.	CTRL+SHIFT+TAB
Go to the next page in the section.	CTRL+PAGE DOWN
Go to the previous page in the section.	CTRL+PAGE UP
Go to the first page in the section.	ALT+HOME
Go to the last page in the section.	ALT+END
Go to the first page in the currently visible set of page tabs.	ALT+PAGE UP
Go to the last page of the currently visible set of page tabs.	ALT+PAGE DOWN
Move or copy the current page.	CTRL+ALT+M
Put focus on the current page tab.	CTRL+ALT+G
Select the current page tab.	CTRL+SHFT+A

Put focus on the current section tab.	CTRL+SHIFT+G
Move the current section.	CTRL+SHIFT+G, and then SHIFT+F10, M
Switch to a different notebook on the Navigation bar.	CTRL+G, then press DOWN ARROW or UP ARROW keys to select a different notebook and then press ENTER
Move the insertion point to the Search box to search all notebooks.	CTRL+E
While searching all notebooks, preview the next result.	DOWN ARROW
While searching all notebooks, go to the selected result and dismiss Search.	ENTER
Change the	CTRL+E, TAB,

search scope.	SPACE
Open the Search Results pane.	ALT+O after searching
Search only the current page. NOTE: You can switch between searching everywhere and searching only the current page at any point by pressing CRTL+E or CTRL+F.	CTRL+F
While searching the current page, move to the next result.	ENTER or F3
While searching the current page, move to the previous result.	SHFT+F3
Dismiss Search and return to the page.	ESC
Move the insertion point to the Search box to search all notebooks.	CTRL+E

While searching all notebooks, preview the next result.	DOWN ARROW
While searching all notebooks, go to the selected result and dismiss Search.	ENTER
Change the search scope.	CTRL+E, TAB, SPACE
Open the Search Results pane.	ALT+O after searching
Search only the current page. NOTE: You can switch between searching everywhere and searching only the current page at any point by pressing CRTL+E or CTRL+F.	CTRL+F
While searching the current page, move to the next result.	ENTER or F3
While searching	SHFT+F3

the current page, move to the previous result.	
Dismiss Search and return to the page.	ESC
Send the selected pages in an e-mail message.	CTRL+SHIFT+E
Send the selected pages in an e-mail message.	CTRL+SHIFT+E
Create a Today Outlook task from the currently selected note.	CTRL+SHIFT+1
Create a Tomorrow Outlook task from the currently selected note.	CTRL+SHIFT+2
Create a This Week Outlook task from the currently selected note.	CTRL+SHIFT+3
Create a Next Week Outlook task from the	CTRL+SHIFT+4

currently selected note.	
Create a No Date Outlook task from the currently selected note.	CTRL+SHIFT+5
Open the selected Outlook task.	CTRL+SHIFT+K
Mark the selected Outlook task as complete.	CTRL+SHIFT+9
Delete the selected Outlook task.	CTRL+SHIFT+0
Show or hide document printouts on the current page (when running OneNote in High Contrast mode).	ALT+SHIFT+P
Insert a picture from a file.	ALT+N, P
Insert a picture from a scanner or a camera.	ALT+N, S
Insert a screen clipping.	Windows logo key+S

NOTE: The OneNote icon must be active in the notification area, at the far right of the Windows taskbar.	
Insert the current date.	ALT+SHIFT+D
Insert the current date and time.	ALT+SHIFT+F
Insert the current time.	ALT+SHIFT+T
Insert a line break.	SHIFT+ENTER
Start a math equation or convert selected text to a math equation.	ALT+=
Insert a Euro (€) symbol.	CTRL+ALT+E
Create a table by adding a second column to already typed text.	TAB
Create another	TAB

column in a table with a single row.	
Create another row when at the end cell of a table. NOTE: Press ENTER a second time to finish the table.	ENTER
Create a row below the current row in a table.	CTRL+ENTER
Create another paragraph in the same cell in a table.	ALT+ENTER
Create a column to the right of the current column in a table.	CTRL+ALT+R
Create a row above the current one in a table (when the cursor is at the beginning of any row).	ENTER
Delete the current empty row in a	DEL (press twice)

table (when the cursor is at the beginning of the row).	
Select all items on the current page. Press CTRL+A more than once to increase the scope of the selection.	CTRL+A
Select to the end of the line.	SHIFT+END
Select the whole line (when the cursor is at the beginning of the line).	SHIFT+DOWN ARROW
Jump to the title of the page and select it.	CTRL+SHIFT+T
Cancel the selected outline or page.	ESC
Move the current paragraph or several selected paragraphs up.	ALT+SHIFT+UP ARROW
Move the current paragraph or	ALT+SHIFT+DO WN ARROW

several selected paragraphs down.	
Move the current paragraph or several selected paragraphs left (decreasing the indent).	ALT+SHIFT+LEF T ARROW
Move the current paragraph or several selected paragraphs right (increasing the indent).	ALT+SHIFT+RIG HT ARROW
Select the current paragraph and its subordinate paragraphs.	CTRL+SHIFT+H YPHEN
Delete the selected note or object.	DELETE
Move to the beginning of the line.	HOME
Move to the end of the line.	END
Move one character to the	LEFT ARROW

left.	
Move one character to the right.	RIGHT ARROW
Go back to the last page visited.	ALT+LEFT ARROW
Go forward to the next page visited.	ALT+RIGHT ARROW
Start playback of a selected audio or video recording.	CTRL+ALT+P or CTRL+ALT+S
Rewind the current audio or video recording by a few seconds.	CTRL+ALT+Y
Fast-forward the current audio or video recording by a few seconds.	CTRL+ALT+U

PS: There's also a shortcut to start OneNote in Windows. Click CTRL+R, type in OneNote and voila. OneNote should open in a jiffy.

Glossary: Keyboard Shortcuts – Mac

This symbol is also known as the Command button. For keyboard shortcuts in which you press two or more keys simultaneously, the keys are separated by a plus sign (+).

To Do This	Press
Select all items on the current page. *NOTE Press Control+A more than once to increase the scope of the selection.*	+ A
Select the page title.	+ Shift + T
Cut the selected text or item.	+ X
Copy the selected text or item to the Clipboard.	+ C
Paste the contents	+ V

of the Clipboard.	
Undo the last action.	+ Z
Redo the last action.	+ Y
Indent a paragraph from the left of a word.	Tab
Indent a paragraph from anywhere in a paragraph.	+]
Remove a paragraph indent from the left.	Shift + Tab or + [
Collapse an expanded outline.	Control + Shift + Plus Sign
Expand a collapsed outline.	Control + Shift + Minus Sign
Open a link.	Return
Copy the format of the selected text.	Option + + C

Paste the copied text format to selected text.	Option + + V
Insert a line break without starting a new paragraph.	Shift + Return
Insert a line break.	Shift + Return
Insert the current date.	+ D
Insert the current date and time.	+ Shift + D
Insert or edit a link.	+ K
Delete the character to the left of the cursor.	Delete
Delete the character to the right of the cursor.	fn + Delete
Delete one word	Option + Delete

to the left.	
Delete one word to the right.	fn + Option +Delete
Move one character to the left.	Left Arrow
Move one character to the right.	Right Arrow
Move one word to the left.	Option +Left Arrow
Move up a line.	Up Arrow
Move down a line.	Down Arrow
Move to the beginning of the line.	+ Left Arrow
Move to the end of the line.	+ Right Arrow
Move to the beginning of the word to the left.	Option + Left Arrow

Move to the ending of the word to the right.	Option + Right Arrow
Go to next paragraph.	+ Up Arrow
Go to the previous paragraph.	+ Down Arrow
Scroll up in the current page.	Page Up
Scroll down in the current page.	Page Down
Go to the top of the page without moving the cursor.	HOME
Go to the bottom of the page without moving the cursor.	END
Go to the next paragraph.	Option + Up Arrow
Go to the previous paragraph.	Option + Down Arrow

Create a table.	Tab
Create another column in a table with a single row.	Tab
Create another row when at the end cell of a table.	Return
NOTE Press Return a second time to finish the table.	
Create a column to the right of the current column in a table.	+ Option+ R
Create a column to the left of the current column in a table.	+ Option + E
Create a row below this one in a table.	+ Return
Create another paragraph in the same cell in a table.	Option + Return

Search on the Page.	+ F
Search all notebooks.	+ Option + F
Switch between sections in a notebook.	Option + Tab
Switch between pages in a section.	1. Start with the cursor within a page, then press Control + Tab.
	2. The focus will move to Add Page, and then press Tab to shift the focus to your pages.
	3. Press Up or Down arrow to select the previous or next page in your section.
Move the current paragraph or several selected paragraphs up.	+ Shift + Up Arrow

Move the current paragraph or several selected paragraphs down.	+ Shift + Down Arrow
Move the current paragraph or several selected paragraphs left (decreasing the indent).	+ Shift + Left Arrow
Move the insertion point up in the current page, or expand the page up.	+ Option + Up Arrow
Move the insertion point down in the current page, or expand the page down.	+ Option + Down Arrow
Move the insertion point left on the current page, or expand the page to the left.	+ Option + Left Arrow

Move the insertion point right in the current page, or expand the page to the right.	+ Option + Right Arrow
Go the place where you can open other notebooks or create new ones.	+ O
View the list of your open notebooks.	Control + G
Create a new notebook page.	+ N
Open the OneNote preferences.	+ , (Comma)
Move the page to another location.	+ Shift + M
Copy page to another location.	+ Shift + C
Move or Copy page again to last	Option + + T

selected section.

Glossary: Math Shortcuts

Arithmetic Operators	What it does
+ *(plus sign)*	Addition
– *(minus sign)*	Subtraction
	Negation
* *(asterisk)*	Multiplication
X (upper- or lowercase x)	Multiplication
/ *(forward slash)*	Division
% *(percent sign)*	Percent
^ *(caret)*	Exponentiation
! *(exclamation)*	Factorial computation

Function	What it does
ABS	Returns the absolute value of a number
ACOS	Returns the arccosine of a number
ASIN	Returns the arcsine of a number
ATAN	Returns the arctangent of a number
COS	Returns the cosine of a number
DEG	Converts an angle (in radians) to degrees
LN	Returns the natural logarithm of a number
LOG	Returns the natural logarithm

	of a number
LOG2	Returns the base-2 logarithm of a number
LOG10	Returns the base-10 logarithm of a number
MOD	Returns remainder of a division operation
PI	Returns the value of π as a constant
PHI	Returns the value of φ (the golden ratio)
PMT	Calculates a loan payment based on a constant interest rate, a constant number of payments, and the present value of the total amount

RAD	Converts an angle (in degrees) to radians
SIN	Returns the sine of the given angle
SQRT	Returns a positive square root
TAN	Returns the tangent of a number

Made in the USA
San Bernardino, CA
24 August 2016